K
F
457
.O3
S29
1995

DEAF Maggie Lee Sayre

D1211045

Media Center (Library)
Elizabethtown Community College
Elizabethtown, KY 42701

$ 20⁰⁰
7/95

'Deaf Maggie Lee Sayre'

Photographs of a River Life

Edited and with an Introduction
by Tom Rankin

University Press of Mississippi
Jackson

Copyright © 1995 by the
University Press of Mississippi
All rights reserved
Manufactured in Korea
by Sung In Printing, Inc.

Designed by John A. Langston

A share of the royalties from the sale of this book
benefit the Maggie Lee Sayre Fund to preserve and
present Ms. Sayre's photographs.

Frontis: "Friends of the Sayre family fishing for
perch and other small fish off the houseboat porch."

CIP Data appear on page 84

For the Sayre family and all those who
choose the river as their home

And for my mother,
Jane Lee Almstedt Rankin

The porch of the Sayre
houseboat from the bank,
1939

Transforming the Familiar

The Photographs of Maggie Lee Sayre

by Tom Rankin

"I shot the flood, all the different scenes, all around the boat," Maggie Lee Sayre recalled, looking at photographs of her family's houseboat. "I really enjoyed that. I wanted to remember how the boat was. There's a picture taken where I'm standing in one boat and I'm shooting the other boat. That was one shot. And the one rowboat was there and I stood there and I shot the big one. I shot the big boat with my camera. Yeah. I stood in the little boat, in the rowboat, and took that shot. Oh, and then I put my camera down and I rowed back to the houseboat. And then I took the film up to Jackson [Tennessee] to the drugstore. Then I got it processed up there."

Photographer Emmet Gowin has argued that "photography is a tool for dealing with things everybody knows about but isn't attending to." The familiar, in other words. There is no better example of a vernacular photographer whose images transform the familiar than Maggie Lee Sayre. For Sayre the camera offered a kind of language—a medium through which she was able to observe, record, and communicate. *Deaf Maggie Lee Sayre* is a book about the origins and nature of individual creativity and communication. The images shown here—images at once personal, cultural, and artistic—are convincing demonstrations of the profound influence of photography on the day-to-day life of an individual who could not hear.

Maggie Lee Sayre, who now lives in a nursing home in Parsons, Tennessee, was born deaf near Paducah, Kentucky, on April 4, 1920. Though the specifics of that day are vague, it seems she entered the world in the small room of a cypress houseboat, one of several built by her father, a fisherman and farmer. She spent much of the next fifty-one years of her life on a river houseboat with her family, who worked as commercial fishermen in Kentucky and Tennessee, along the Ohio and Tennessee Rivers and their tributaries. Sayre inherited the traditional river life of the upland South, a culture defined by the individualistic spirit of houseboat dwellers who lived apart from those in conventional land-based society. Isolated by choice, the Sayres moved frequently, seeking the ideal river landing. Maggie, unable to hear or speak, was a quiet yet perceptive participant in the life and work of her parents.

When she was sixteen or eighteen years old—the exact year is difficult to pinpoint—Maggie Sayre acquired a simple Kodak box camera. Using black-and-white film, she began photographing her family, friends, and scenes in her river-world surroundings. Her pictures document a traditional river culture that is rooted in subsistence living.

But more than that, the camera allowed her to broaden her communicative skills and to find meaning and power in visual expression. The act of taking pictures expanded her opportunities for a dialogue with a hearing world. Although she was entirely untrained in photography, her pictures reveal a personal aesthetic that evolved as a response to her deafness, to her environment, and to her belief in the value of collecting visual images of ordinary life. If her photographs, expressive and compelling in any context, are intimate documents of a fading traditional life-style, they are also the creative response of a woman who spent over fifty years on a riverboat unable to hear or communicate verbally with her parents and friends.

In 1982 I was photographing and interviewing river families and fishermen along the lower Tennessee River with folklorist and naturalist Bob Fulcher; we were working on a project sponsored by the Department of Conservation to build an interpretive center of Tennessee River folk culture. Interested in the full range of that culture, we asked a number of people along the Tennessee River about houseboat dwellers and where we might locate families still living on boats. Over the years, locals told us, most of the houseboat families had either moved off the Tennessee River or been forced to leave by the Tennessee Valley Authority, which controlled a large section of the river after the building of the dams. The Sayres, mentioned repeatedly by people we met, were one of the few families who had continued to live on their houseboat into the 1970s. It seemed that they were not only more stubborn and committed than others but were sometimes all too willing to fight for what they saw as their natural right to live on the river. The Tennessee Valley Authority officials, one person recalled, eventually understood this and gave up on moving Mr. Sayre from the river, allowing him and his daughter Maggie to continue to live on their houseboat.

Bob Fulcher and I tracked down the Sayre boat in late 1982; it was near the Tennessee River on a piece of land off Brodie Road in Decatur County, approximately eighty miles west of Nashville. We found a woman living nearby who had known the Sayre family and had visited them during the time they lived on the river. She encouraged us to visit the nursing home several miles away in Parsons and talk to Maggie Lee Sayre, the only remaining member of the family. Maggie Lee Sayre, she told us, might have some old pictures.

Bob Fulcher and I went to see Maggie Sayre on a Sunday evening in December 1982. We met her in the reception area of the small nursing home, where other residents sat, clustered in their wheelchairs, competing for our attention. In a short, handwritten note, we explained to Miss Sayre our purpose in coming. Motioning for us to sit on the sofa, she disappeared down a hall. Bob and I

Maggie Lee Sayre with her camera, Decatur County, Tennessee, 1987. © Tom Rankin

noticed that a number of the other residents of Decatur County Manor were very old, and that some were clearly senile and probably dependent on twenty-four-hour care. It seemed to us that Maggie did not need such care or deserve such isolation. Several minutes later she returned with two large photo albums, one dating from the late 1930s. Seated on the sofa between Bob and me, Maggie showed us her life in pictures. In written notes, she explained that, after her father's death in 1977, she had gone to live with her uncle Ted and aunt Pansy in Cadiz, Kentucky. After a few days, she recalled, her uncle Ted had brought her to the nursing home, where she has been since. "They really didn't want to take care of me," she explained several years later. "They put me in the [nursing] home."

We spent a long time with Maggie Lee Sayre that night. Communicating in words only through short notes, we mostly learned about her from her photographs. She accepted us with gracious hospitality and trust. We often stumbled in our attempts to ask questions clearly, but Maggie exhibited patience, appreciation, and brisk humor. Even with the communication difficulties, we had a productive visit, during which we were able to determine the basic outline of Maggie's story through her picture albums. Finding the photographs extraordinary, I knew that I wanted to see more, to learn more about the Sayres' houseboat life and Maggie's personal chronicle of it. As we were leaving, I asked if she might take time to sit down and write a short life story for us. We told her we would come again the next week to continue our visit.

When we returned a week later, she presented us with one typewritten page describing her life:

Maggie Lee Sayre was born to Archie and May Sayre on April 4, 1920. They had another daughter, Myrtle. They lived in a 3 room houseboat on Click Creek, Paducah, Kentucky. Maggie and Myrtle were deaf when born.

Archie was a fisherman. He made nets with twine and put them in the river. He waited 2 days and then rode the motorboat down the river to raise the nets. He caught cat, buffalo, and carp. He used snag lines to catch spoonbills and catfish. He was a good fisherman. May liked to fish off the porch. She baited her hooks with worms.

When Maggie was 7 years old and Myrtle was 8 years old, Pauline Roth sent them to a school for the deaf in Danville, Kentucky. She gave them clothes to wear. They stayed 9 months and came back home for June, July and August. They rode a train from Paducah to Danville.

After school, the family moved to Smithland, KY. Archie and helper Charles East fished. They baited the trot lines with carp meat. In the evenings put the trot lines in the river.

They put 8 or 10 lines in at one time. They usually caught catfish. They sold all kinds of fish to a market in Paducah, KY. They enjoyed eating fish at home anytime. May cooked breakfast at 6:00 am each morning so they could leave early to fish.

When Myrtle was 16 years old, May went in to wake her for breakfast, but Myrtle had died during the night. Her body was brought to Lindsey's Funeral Home, Paducah, KY. Archie called some family members and they came to visit them. The family moved back to Paducah. Mrs. Roth sent Maggie back to school in Danville. She stayed there until she was 19 years old. Archie and May met her at the depot and they all returned home and were very happy.

They moved to the Tennessee River. They sailed the houseboat and motor boat to Tom Creek. They stayed there for 3 years. They continued to sell fish to a market. They then moved to

Click Creek near Sugar Tree, TN. After that they moved to several places down the Tennessee River and stayed a few weeks in one place.

They decided they liked Click Creek best, so they moved back. Maggie's mother got sick and was took to Jackson Hospital.

She later died. She was buried in Paducah, KY.

The houseboat was getting old, so they moved to a house on Brodie Road. This was in 1971. Archie liked to hunt and they enjoyed eating ducks, squirrel and rabbits.

Archie became sick and had to stop fishing in 1974. He died March, 1977. Maggie went home with her Uncle Ted and Aunt Pansy for a few days. They then brought her to Decatur County Nursing Home, which later moved and was named Decatur County Manor Nursing Center. Her uncle and aunt visit whenever possible.

She signed her life story "Deaf Maggie Lee Sayre."

Although the Sayre family's life-style might have seemed unusual to their land-based neighbors in McCracken County, Kentucky, in the 1920s, they were actually part of a large community of houseboat dwellers along the Ohio and Tennessee Rivers. Throughout the South many families lived on the river. Ben Lucien Burman, writing for the *Saturday Evening Post* in 1938 in an article titled "Shanty Boat Coming Down," estimated that as many as thirty thousand houseboats dotted the many rivers and creeks of the region. Burman's descriptions of the culture, though tainted with the pejorative class-conscious stereotyping of the day, stressed the isolation and individualistic freedom of houseboat dwellers. The river dwellers lived on a "frontier," Burman contended, which "passes within a few hundred feet of some of the

great inland cities of America, but the nation as a whole knows less of the shantymen who form such a picturesque segment of its population than it knows of the natives in Bali."

Drawing parallels between "shantymen" and the Balinese was rare indeed; however, most writers and observers did choose to characterize the river people as "river rats" and the river families' homes as "shanties" rather than "houseboats," the term preferred by Maggie Lee Sayre and other river dwellers. Sayre denies ever having lived on a "shantyboat"; however, she is willing and proud to share memories of her houseboat life. Folklorist Jens Lund has written that use of the term "shantyboat" may indicate a negative attitude toward these families, including the notion of a stereotypical houseboater who is a lazy, dishonest thief.

Artist and writer Harlan Hubbard, a Kentuckian, described the houseboat life-style in his classic, if romantic, *Shantyboat, A River Way of Life*, published in 1953:

The true shantyboater has a purer love for the river than had his drifting flatboat predecessors. These were concerned with trade of new land. To him the river is more than a means of livelihood. It is a way of life, the only one he knows which answers his innate longing to be untrammeled and independent, to live on the fringe of society, almost beyond the law, beyond taxes and ownership of property. His drifting downstream is as natural to him as his growing old in the stream of time. Away from the river he languishes, as if taken from his natural element.

Hubbard went on to say that the "art of drifting" downstream had become a thing of the past, as those who lived on houseboats acquired motors or smaller push boats equipped with motors. He was writing in the 1940s, when, in fact, many were taking advantage of the additional freedoms offered by the gas-powered motor. From his earliest river days, Archie Sayre used a boat motor on a small john boat to push his larger houseboat. His pattern, rather than drifting downstream, was to head upstream.

Whatever the method of transport, the houseboat represented the consummate river life-style in the South. Up until the 1950s families living seminomadic lives could be seen on a variety of houseboat constructions on the Mississippi, Tennessee, Ohio, Cumberland, and other southern rivers and tributaries. Though portrayed by the popular media as impoverished, lawless "water gypsies," these river folk often made conscious choices to pursue lives of mobility. Although the Depression years swelled the ranks of river folk, as many southerners were compelled by economic hardship to find alternative sources of income, food and shelter, many had chosen such a life earlier in the century, opting to make livelihoods fishing, trapping, rafting logs, and musseling.

Archie Sayre certainly made a personal decision to move onto the river. Born into a farm family in McCracken County, Kentucky, Sayre grew up working on his father's farm. The Sayres' sixty-acre farm, however, bordered Clarks River, which flows into the Ohio River at Paducah. Ted Sayre, Archie's brother, recalls Archie's move from land to water: "Whenever we owned this farm, why, Archie's wife's father lived on our place on a houseboat. You know what I mean, tied to the bank. And Archie got acquainted with them. And that's how come, Arch, he just took up the river."

Archie may have "took up the river" in part because when he was seventeen or eighteen he married the daughter, May, of the houseboat family that was tied to the bank bordering the Sayres' farm. It is not clear whether Archie and May Sayre ever lived on anything other than a houseboat

after their marriage. Ted Sayre remembers them living on a "dry docked houseboat" for several years, and by 1920 they were on a floating houseboat. May Sayre's parents, says Ted, were both "river people," who had come downstream to Paducah from Johnsonville, Tennessee, on the Tennessee River. Ironically, Archie and May Sayre later moved just upriver from the old town of Johnsonville, which had been covered by water when the TVA built Kentucky Lake.

Although May Sayre's river background might have influenced Archie, he also had the tradition of river work running through his own family. Along with working the farm, Archie's father ran a supply boat and ferry across the Clarks River. "That may have been where he [Archie] picked it up at," considered Ted Sayre. Both Ted Sayre and Archie Sayre tried their hands at commercial fishing while they were young farmhands.

From interviews with Maggie and with Ted Sayre, it is clear that Archie built at least two houseboats: a two-room boat made sometime between 1910 and 1920 and a three-room boat built in the early 1920s. The three-room vessel, a sixty-foot cypress boat, is the one that Maggie lived on and the one she frequently photographed. The smaller boat became Archie Sayre's father's house. The sixty-foot boat was undoubtedly one of the biggest handmade houseboats on either the Ohio River or the Tennessee River, and Maggie has clear memories of her old home:

My father made the boat. He did it himself. I was a baby. And this was in Paducah, Kentucky. He worked slow and built the boat. It's a three-room boat. There's a bedroom, and there's another very small room and then there's a larger room. We had a dresser and my father's bed was in the first room and then a closet in the first room. And in my father's room there's a sewing machine, a

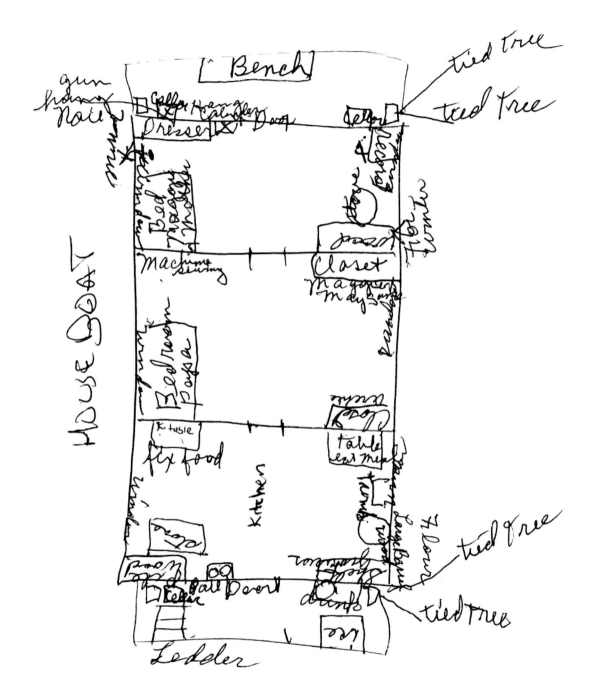

Houseboat floorplan drawn
by Maggie Lee Sayre and
Bob Fulcher

The sixty-foot houseboat built by Archie Sayre

little treadle sewing machine. And then in the front room, the third room, there's the kitchen area where we had a stove. And there's a table where we make the food, we cut things up, we make biscuits, we mix things up and cook. And then we'd take that food, whatever we were mixing and put it over on the stove. We had a box outside for ice. And back on the corner we had a container with water. We drank water from a creek. It was nice water. A spring. My father had a big, big jar that he used for water.

Clearly Archie Sayre had the river in his blood. He grew up near the river and married a woman from a river family. He took to the river very early, perhaps because of his desire for independence. When other commercial fishermen along the Tennessee River speak of Archie Sayre, their voices hold an echo of fear and intimidation; they remember him as a fine fisherman and whiskey maker but also as a man who was often caustic and violent. T. J. Whitfield, a commercial fisher-

man and musseler from Holladay in Benton County, Tennessee, remembered several incidents in which Archie Sayre showed his shotgun to commercial fishermen who entered fishing waters he thought of as his. Whitfield's stories and numerous others challenge the romantic portrayal of a delicate and sensitive family choosing to live on the free-flowing waters of nature. Even today as Maggie Lee Sayre expresses her love and respect for her father, she also recalls the pain wrought by his quick anger, frequent harshness, and insensitivity. Whether Archie Sayre coveted the isolation he created for his family to avoid the larger, more encumbered world is not clear, but it does seem that he needed independence, freedom, and control, all of which came with a life on upland rivers in the South.

The Sayre boat was extremely durable; it floated in Kentucky and then in Tennessee until 1971 when the TVA used a highway department tractor to drag it for nearly a mile down a gravel road, where it remained until someone burned it in 1994. Even when it was abandoned and beginning to rot, the strength and beauty of its construction continued to be apparent.

Typically a houseboat family would find a safe, fertile place to tie up, perhaps at the mouth of a small tributary, where the boat would be shielded from major wakes and other disturbances of river traffic. A garden planted in the summer might provide vegetables that could then be canned for use during the cold months. Hunting and trapping yielded food and cash throughout the winter for many river families. Fish, however, was both the major "cash crop" and the family staple; not surprisingly, Maggie Sayre remembers eating fish nearly every day of her fifty-one years on the river. Commercial fishermen employed a variety of tackle to catch fish, including trot lines, snag lines, barrel nets, gill nets, trammel nets, and wooden fish traps. If a particular landing was suitable, a family might stay for a few years or longer; if not, they would quickly relocate to a safer, more productive spot on the river.

Though the Sayres did not move as frequently as some houseboat families, they did live at a number of different river landings. From Maggie's birthplace on Clarks River, Archie and May moved the boat over to Smithland, Kentucky. Their major move, however, was from Smithland up the Tennessee River in 1939 or 1940. Maggie remembers that it took her family a while to find a permanent landing. "We didn't stay in one place," she said of their move up the Tennessee River. "We were in Perryville [Tennessee]. And after Perryville we went down to Pickwick Dam, then back to the Perryville bridge. But we didn't stay there long because the musselers dragged the area and broke my father's nets. We also lived at Tom Creek, but this [Click Creek] was the best place.

We stayed here a long time." The "best place" was at the mouth of Click Creek near Sugar Tree, Tennessee, in Decatur County. They stayed at that landing until Maggie and her father moved off the river in 1971.

Maggie Sayre and her older sister Myrtle were both born deaf. Separated by one year in age, they were very close friends and shared intimate times during their early years near Paducah. No one in the family is sure of the cause of their deafness, though Ted Sayre remembers Archie taking the two girls to a Paducah hearing specialist who attempted to help them with hearing aids. Nothing ever worked satisfactorily, however. Ted recalls Maggie refusing to wear her "hear phones" because "she said they hurt her head." "He [Archie] spent a lot of money on both of them," says Ted. "Fact of the business is when Myrtle was little I imagine he spent just about all he made except what he eat. I stayed with Archie whenever they was small. Some. And they'd [Maggie and

May Sayre, Maggie Sayre's mother, fishing from houseboat porch

14

Myrtle] be a setting down playing, with their backs towards me, but you couldn't slip up on them. And they couldn't hear or talk. But you couldn't slip up on them. They'd turn around and see you."

Maggie remembers her early childhood days with Myrtle when they played on and near the houseboat. "We could gesture," she recalls. "But it [our ability to talk] wasn't fast when we were little. When we were five or six. Our talking was very slow." Using gestures only, they would play the days away, often with a doll of Myrtle's. Together they would make clothes for the doll just as their mother made clothes for them. With no other houseboat families near them, each was the other's only playmate.

Like many deaf children in the rural South, Maggie and Myrtle were left to themselves by family members who understood little about their deafness, their needs, or what the educational possibilities were. A local funeral home owner, however, took an abiding interest in the two Sayre girls and somehow arranged for them to attend Kentucky School for the Deaf (KSD) in Danville, Kentucky. Pauline Roth, who was in the funeral home business with her brother, had grown up an orphan. She was generous and concerned, remembers Ted Sayre: "They found out that he had these two girls that couldn't hear or talk and they come out and seen Archie. And the lady Roth seen after them. And Arch put money in the bank in Paducah and she could check it out for the girls. This woman seen that she caught that train to Danville and bought the clothes. Archie gave her the money to buy the clothes, give her rights to write a check and ever what she needed in school." While Archie Sayre may have set up an account at the local bank, it is evident from what others remember that Pauline Roth used her money to help educate the two Sayre girls. When Maggie, seven, and Myrtle, eight, went off to school, it was the beginning of a profound broadening of experience in their lives. At Kentucky School for the Deaf they met other deaf students, lived in dormitories with other girls, studied writing, reading, mathematics, and home economics, and learned sign language. Meeting other deaf children let Maggie know that she and Myrtle were not alone. Learning sign language gave both girls a way to communicate further with each other as well as with their newfound friends in Danville.

Maggie Lee Sayre remembers her first trip to Danville, in 1927, as disorienting. She boarded the train at Paducah with absolutely no idea where she was going. She did not know sign language and could not read; there was no way for her to understand anyone's explanation of where she was going or for what purpose. She must have wondered if she would ever come back. Mildred Middleton, another deaf student, rode the train from Paducah to KSD with Maggie Sayre that year. Middleton described her first trip as unnerving: "They put me on the train and I looked at my mother and daddy and I just waved. Don't know where I was going." The train traveled through western Kentucky from Paducah to Union Station in Louisville, where students changed trains for the trip from Louisville to Danville. A four-hour wait greeted them in Louisville. By now there was a group of deaf children waiting together. The older ones, familiar with sign language and with each other, talked and reminisced together. New students making their first trip, who still understood little of what was happening, could only observe curiously, mystified by the constant hand motions just as they were by other people's mouths moving incessantly. For the Sayre girls, the strangeness of their surroundings was magnified because of the

Two pages from Maggie Lee Sayre's photo albums, date 1937 and 1938. The top page depicts her mother's life on the houseboat, her father as a fisherman, and Maggie's friends at the Union Station in Lousiville, KY, in route to Kentucky School for the Deaf in Danville. The bottom page contrasts Maggie's two worlds: the river and Kentucky School for the Deaf.

rural, subsistence nature of their life. Here were two girls from a houseboat near Paducah sitting in the bustling interior of Union Station as L&N locomotives moved in and out.

Maggie and Myrtle did not arrive in Danville until midnight, at which time they had a one-mile ride from the train depot to the KSD campus. "The funny thing about that is when I got off, when we children got off from Danville at the depot, all the way to school is one mile," recalls Mildred Middleton. "From the depot. And we rode in the wagon with the mule. That's what they carried us in from the depot to the School for the Deaf." When the wagon reached campus the girls were shown to their beds in the "little girls' cottage," where Maggie settled on the first floor in a room with thirty-two beds. Maggie's housemother, Olive Giovannoli, known to students as "Miss Olive," welcomed her.

Miss Olive may have been the first person to give Maggie and other new students their names. Making a sign for "M" and holding it close to her chest, she showed Maggie her "name sign." Probably as she learned the rudiments of sign language, Maggie would say, "My name [is] Maggie Lee Sayre," using finger spelling, and then follow the spelling of her name with her name sign. This sign was what everyone at KSD would use. For the first time in her seven years, Maggie Lee Sayre could see that she had a name. Her parents had simply summoned her through gesture; nothing so personal as a name had ever been used. And while they and others on the river would continue to rely on gesture for communication with Maggie, the girl now had a recognizable name sign that was hers and hers alone. It was the beginning of her development of an individual identity within the deaf community at KSD.

When Maggie and Myrtle entered KSD in 1927,

there were two different types of classes, manual and oral. Oral classes were for some students who could learn to read lips and voice sounds and would therefore be able to live and work in a hearing world. In manual classes, sign language was taught to those students who did not seem able to succeed in oral classes. Maggie was placed in the manual class.

Maggie has fond memories of her school days in Danville and of her trips back and forth on the train. She stayed at KSD for a full nine months each year, going back home only during the summers. During her twelve years at the school, her parents never visited her in Danville. She spent all holidays with her friends at KSD. Holidays were special times for the children, and the school fostered a close feeling of family among the students, teachers, housemothers and housefathers. Over fifty years after leaving KSD in 1940, Maggie still refers to it as a "very special school."

Clearly Maggie's experience at the school and her relationships with other deaf students contrasted sharply with her unique home life on the river. Maggie moved from the outdoor world of the houseboat and commercial fishing to a world of brick buildings and chalkboards. At home she had no community of friends her age and no one with whom she could sign. This transition from river life to school life offered her a fresh perspective on her deafness and on her family's river existence. A page from her earliest scrapbook clearly illustrates her two worlds: her life on the river where she spent three months each summer, and her life at school where she spent the other nine months with friends in dormitories and classrooms. Though a mere train ride apart, Maggie's experience in the two places was vastly different. Her time at KSD, I believe, enabled her to observe the houseboat life with both the detachment of an outsider and the intimacy of a participant. For a dozen years she spent more time in Danville than on the boat with her parents; this time away surely increased her sensitivity to the mystery found in the day-to-day patterns of river life.

Maggie's first camera entered the Sayre family through a national public relations program sponsored by Eastman Kodak Company in 1930, the company's fiftieth anniversary year. Kodak gave free cameras to children who turned twelve years old in 1930, ordinarily distributing them through Kodak dealers. Mr. Lee, superintendent at Kentucky School for the Deaf, wrote to Kodak requesting that cameras come to KSD directly for his twelve-year-old students. Mr. T. H. McCabe, a representative from Eastman Kodak's service department, answered Lee's letter promptly:

> *Certainly the gift cameras and film should be made as easy as possible for the children in your institution of eligible age to obtain.*
>
> *Although our regular method of distributing the gifts is through dealers, we know that in many cases it would be impossible for a child to go to a store, hence we are glad to make an exception and send the cameras directly to you.*
>
> *If our little gift brings a ray of happiness to children who receive it, you may be sure that it will add to our happiness also.*

A 1930 issue of *The Kentucky Standard*, KSD's school newsletter, published the names of the thirty children who received cameras. Myrtle Sayre, who had been born on September 3, 1918, received one of those cameras. When Myrtle died unexpectedly six years later, Maggie inherited the camera.

Fellow classmates remember Myrtle as often sick and prone to epileptic seizures. Whatever her actual condition, Myrtle was not well and died suddenly on New Year's Day in 1936. Maggie remembers the details of the day:

> *Myrtle was in good health at first, but at the age of sixteen when we were in Smithland, Kentucky, she got sick. She was okay for awhile, but then my father was out helping a man named Charles East fish and I was doing some cleaning and what happened was that just after a few months it seemed that my sister was not well.*
>
> *And one night she was in bed and she had been feeling very chilled and we put the quilts on top of her. Then by the next morning when my mother came in to wake her up—actually my father had already gone to work, to fish, and my mother had already cooked the breakfast—she walked into the bedroom and tapped my sister to get up, but she just never woke up. And so my mother went and called my father and he got things going and came on in on the boat and we all got dressed up and took my sister to the funeral home in Paducah. And we called all the other relatives together and she was buried.*
>
> *And then I was the only one after the age of fifteen to go to school. Prior to that time my sister and I would travel together to school and be together. But after the age of fifteen until the age of nineteen I went to school alone.*

With Myrtle's death, Maggie lost not only her traveling companion but also her closest friend and the only person on the houseboat with whom she could use sign language, which had become her primary mode of communication. Maggie was now almost completely isolated from other deaf people while she was at home on the river. Communication with her parents, whose reading and writing skills were limited, consisted of short notes written on a small pad of paper that Maggie always carried with her and of a well-developed and effective set of gestures and home signs.

Although Maggie had lost her sister and main

confidant, she inherited what would become another good friend—the small Kodak box camera that Myrtle had been given. Maggie remembers it as a "tan camera" that was bigger than a Kodak she had later. She began using the camera immediately. "Maggie was so excited about her pictures," Middleton recalls. "She always carried them at school." Other students also had cameras and exchanged pictures to put in their scrapbooks and memory albums. But it was Maggie's river pictures that she was most excited about. Willie Leona Coles, a reporter for the "From the Girls' Side" column in *The Kentucky Standard*, wrote about Maggie's pictures in the September 30, 1937, issue:

> *Maggie Sayre has a picture of her father with a big fish. Maggie said that her father is fond of fishing and often goes out on the water for several days. Her father was very lucky because he caught a fish that weighed fifty-three pounds.*

Maggie later remarked, "I used the pictures to show people so they would enjoy it. My snapshots. But other pictures that I could have, that I could keep for myself and remember, I took them to school. For several years I took pictures all the time, all the time. Of different things around." Her photo albums are a record not only of her river life but include photographs she took at school and in commercial studios and photo booths. Pictures of herself appear frequently in the albums. When asked why she took certain pictures throughout her life, she most often responds by saying simply, "I want to remember."

There is a question as to whether any of the pictures were taken by Myrtle Sayre. The tan Kodak camera was hers for six years. Maggie remembers her using the camera but has no clear recall of Myrtle's photographs. The possibility exists that a few of the earliest photographs in Maggie Sayre's photo album were actually taken by her sister; if so, Maggie does not remember which ones. The tan camera, once a central instrument in Maggie's response to the world around her, is no longer with her. Sometime in the late 1950s or early 1960s, acquiring film for the camera began to be difficult. Maggie finally went to a drugstore near Click Creek in Decatur County, Tennessee, and bought a new Kodak Duaflex II. She describes her usual procedure in working: "I bought this camera at a drugstore in Parsons [Tennessee]. After I took the pictures I mailed the film to Jackson to be processed. It would take a week or so to get the pictures back. I would get the mail at my neighbor's house. Some of the pictures would be good, some fair, some okay." She still has the Duaflex II, keeping it in the original box.

One of the earliest photographs that Maggie took, in 1937, is a portrait of her father cleaning a hoop net. Explaining the significance of the net-cleaning activity, she reveals her roles both as participant in the family river economy and as observer with a camera. This duality—participant and observer, insider and outsider—is central to the nature of Sayre's work. Her ability to view ordinary activity as important and valuable photographic subject matter is in part a result of her school days in Danville, where she gained an outsider's perspective on her houseboat life.

As Archie Sayre fished and cleaned nets, so did Maggie. She had her own boat; she made and repaired trot lines, snag lines and nets; she cleaned the commercial fishing tackle her father used: "I would help row and pull the lines in. I would help make the dip nets, I did those. I watched my father and I picked it up from him. The dip nets. We had two different sizes. I didn't lift the [hoop] nets. The trot lines I could pull in, but I couldn't lift the nets. They were much too heavy, much too heavy for me to pull out of the

water. But I could pull the trot lines." She sold the fish she caught, and the money she made was hers to spend as she wished. Often she used it to buy film and pay for film processing. She also kept sales accounts for the family, calculating how much the fish weighed and how much money was due from the buyers. In these various ways, Maggie was thoroughly involved in the day-to-day economy of commercial fishing.

So the photographs—over 250 of them—chroni-cle her family's life on the river in a series of ordi-nary, daily activities. Using a conventional box camera, she photographed scenes she saw regular-ly, such as her father with his daily catch or her mother sitting on the porch of the houseboat fishing. When the spring floods came and disrupt-ed the quiet boat tied to the bank, or when winter ice threatened the very foundation of her family's home, Maggie responded by taking pictures. When her father pulled a fifty-pound catfish from a snag

Series of photographs depict-ing the process of tarring hoop nets

20

line, Maggie offered congratulations and fixed the scene in memory by taking a picture.

Nothing was too quiet, too mundane for a photograph. Speaking about a simple portrait of her mother on the houseboat porch, Maggie explains what she sees in the image: "This is my mother. She enjoyed standing there, just watching, looking out over the dock. She liked to fish every day. She also just like to look at the river and look for fish. She cooked. She sewed. I made trot lines and dip nets and set up all the snag lines and cleaned them so they were nice and clean."

Like this description of May Sayre, Maggie's other photographs contain for her the symbolic narratives of her life.

One of her favorite photographic subjects was the big fish. "I shot the fish," she once commented. "And I really enjoyed when we had those big fish. So I shot the big fish. I didn't usually shoot the small fish, just the bigger ones. I liked that, it was a good time." In addition to shooting the big fish herself, she occasionally drafted her father to photograph her with the fish. These pictures are compelling for their subject matter alone, as Maggie recognizes. But a big fish was more than just a good photo opportunity; it was, for the Sayres, better pay for the same work. Archie Sayre fished every day. Some days he caught very little and some days more, but when a fish weighed anywhere near fifty pounds it was cause for celebration. Maggie recorded these triumphs with pictures. "When we caught a large fish I'd take a picture before it was sold," she once explained. "Then I could remember the big fish hanging on the scale." Expressions of her attention to family, work, and home, Maggie's photographs are personal in the truest sense. Her pictures transform the ordinary into the extraordinary.

Her desire to execute simple, clear documenta-tion of her father's work is obvious from a series of pictures she took of Archie and a friend tarring hoop nets. Before the advent of nylon line, commercial fisherman had to tar their nets regularly to prevent rotting of the cotton line. This is a process Maggie saw countless times and occasionally helped with. Her documenting of such a routine task indicates how important she felt everyday activity was to the telling of her story. Presenting the four pictures as a series in her photograph album, she describes the major stages of net tarring: "This is a series of pictures. The second one you see there is a helper helping my father. And the helper's name is Charles East. Charles is hoisting the net up out of the tar. And then on the third picture down here you see how long the net is when it's strung out. And then the fourth picture over there is dragging the nets along and setting them to the side." This series suggests the photographer's intentionally documentary approach to the family's work culture. An outsider observing the Sayres' boat in the 1930s could hardly have produced a more thorough series of documentary photographs.

The Sayres' houseboat was a center of activity, with community members visiting often, swapping stories, fishing off the porch of the houseboat, or exchanging commercial fishing information. When visitors came, Maggie often photographed them. Since she seldom went anywhere, these visitors were her main connection with a larger world.

Like other collections of family photographs—and these are just that—Maggie Sayre's pictures present us with a somewhat idealized view of her river world. While we do not see repeated images of holidays or of birthdays and other rites of passage as we do in most family collections—the Sayres did not do much of that sort of celebrating—Maggie did tend to emphasize the happy moments: friends and relatives visiting, fish and turtles freshly caught, the simple beauty of the river landscape, the family at its center. If, as Susan Sontag says, photographs are "experience captured," Sayre's pictures indicate a generally pleasant life.

But photography served multiple purposes for Maggie Lee Sayre. First, she could engage in a dialogue with family members and visitors by taking their portraits. Second, she was able to define and represent her world as she saw it (or wanted to see it) and thus find her own place in it. And finally, by editing and organizing her small black-and-white prints in well-conceived, carefully planned photo albums, often with added text and dates, she created a pictorial narrative analogous to an oral autobiography. Turning the pages of her photo books, she reveals the story of her life, of her family, and of the river. Her pictures exist simultaneously as autobiography, regional reflection, cultural document, and story. For a woman unable to hear or speak, the medium of photography offered a poignant communicative device that provided an escape from isolation. Entirely self-taught, Maggie photographed as instinct directed, following Kodak's cardinal rule of exposure by trying to keep the sun behind her when taking a portrait. The subtleties within her photographs are the result of a rare confluence of factors: her deafness, her fifty-one years on the river, her intimate knowledge of the work and life of commercial fishing.

Her actual life and the life portrayed in her photographs were very much the same. She saw the people and places she photographed day after day, night after night. Born into the traditional river culture, living it, and helping to shape it, she made a pictorial narrative of family, place, work, and life that is a self-portrait and at the same time documentation and dialogue with those around

her. Maggie's river life was a sheltered life. She seldom wandered far from the houseboat or the river, particularly after she quit going to Kentucky School for the Deaf in 1940. Though occasionally exposed to the unpredictability of the natural world and the vicissitudes of self-sufficiency, she lived for the most part in isolated circumstances where little changed from day to day. Danville was as far from home as she ever went. Her world was the world of the houseboat and the small river communities where the boat was tied.

Through the photographs, however, she was able to broaden and magnify that world and to share her place with others. Maggie Sayre found an appropriate and effective medium that allowed her to articulate her feelings about where she lived and that gave her a way to remember. She discovered a more vital and expressive life by telling her story through photographic images. Maggie Lee Sayre reflects the truth told by Eudora Welty, who, commenting on her own sheltered early life, said, "A sheltered life can be a very daring life. For all serious daring starts from within."

DEAF Maggie Lee Sayre

View of the Sayre house-
boat from the bank, July
1939, Smithland Ken-
tucky

Page from Maggie Lee Sayre's scrapbook, July 1938, Smithland, Kentucky

26

My father, Archie Sayre, in 1937. This is where he is shaking to get the leaves out, to get them out of the net. Also, he's got a brush to keep them clean. You see here, he's got a rope and he'll have a rock attached to the rope and he'll wash them. I was standing at his back, looking at him. I snapped it as he raised the net. He didn't know, he didn't see me. I was just kind of standing there, he didn't look back.

This is my mother, May
Sayre, in 1937.

Dog coming up plank, May 1940, Paducah, Kentucky

▶

Butch sitting up on the houseboat porch. Wood is piled on bench to keep it dry in winter snow, and we needed wood to stay warm.

This place was Maggie Bawcum's place. This is me, right here. Maggie Bawcum took care of mail for my family. We'd wait a while, maybe 10 o'clock and I'd walk and get the mail. It was a man named Jackson who agreed to shoot the picture with my camera. You see the tire for flowers in the back, it was really nice. I could walk from Click Creek around to there. I'd walk it.

The woman who helped
Tom and Bobby find me
gave me this picture.
This is me. That's my
mother and father. That
mirror is for shaving.
And then there was a
dresser on the side.
I always wore dresses.
Except when it was very
cold. I had one pair of
jeans for when it was
very cold. And I wore
them when I went out to
get wood for the fire. I
wore leather boots.

Page from Sayre scrapbook, 1948

This is my father on the left with Robert Haynes. He works at the market. And this is where my father is selling fish to Robert. Sometimes he would come every two or three weeks, but if there were many fish he would come more often. Spring there would be a lot of fish. And fall too. Summer was too hot. Winter was just too cold. There were very few in winter. Very few.

Archie Sayre and friends Sam and Maggie Baw-cum on our dock. They stood to hold big catfish together at Click Creek landing.

My father caught that fish. I was there for fun. I showed my father how to use the camera. I showed him how to set it and my father snapped the picture. I showed him how to look into it and he saw that it was o.k. It's kind of pretty. That fish weighed 75 maybe, I don't know.

This is when fish were all ready. And he had to go around the other side and get them for Robert Haynes so Robert could take them in the truck. And then they'd be weighed and sold. We'd keep fish in the live box my father built for two or three weeks sometimes. In the big box. They'd be alive in there. These fish were in the box. They came from the nets and went into the box. And then all of these were sold. I came down off the porch. I told him, wait. Before you go and sell those fish I want to snap the shot. I want to show that we have all these fish. So I held up my camera and I said wait until I snap this. And I did and he took his boat around. I'd just kind of motion to him to hang on and he'd understand me.

This was at Tom Creek in Tennessee. That's where this was taken. That's a wash tub. This is Mary Lou, Charles, and Warren.

I told them to wait and look at me and then I snapped the shot. Yea, I showed them the picture later. It's very dark, hard to see, but there's a net back in the trees, a hoop net. Hung there to dry out. They needed to dry out after they'd been dyed. We'd let them dry two or three days before we'd put them back in the river.

This might have been before the dog house. He was on land. This was in Smithland, Kentucky. He just had a barrel in Smithland. When we got Butch as a puppy, my father would train him to sit up and he would sit up. And after a while, after he'd grown, he could do it pretty well. And all I had to do was motion to him and he would sit up like this. The barrel is where he slept.

Me on houseboat porch
with a young boy

▶

This is my mother. This
is while she was resting,
just looking out. I told
her I was going to snap
the picture, stay put.
You can see here, she'd
got these wire snipers.
Remember I told you
about the wire sniper.
And this is the saw.
That's the box. It wasn't
really nice, but you sit
on it while you were
fishing. She was rest-
ing. She liked the pic-
ture. The tire was so the
dock wouldn't bang
against the porch.

See, he's got water in
there. He's got a lot of
water in there and he's
using this pail to get the
water out. And there
are fish in there and
he'll put the fish in
there and take fish out.
He's using this scoop.

   To get his attention,
I didn't touch him. I
waved to him and he'd
stand there and I took
the picture.

Uncle Ted Sayre, Cousin William Weber, his son Warren, Aunt Pansy Sayre, Maggie Lee Sayre, Archie Sayre, May Sayre. Photograph was taken by cousin Ruth Weber.

Aunt Rose Byrd, Mrs.
May Sayre, and Lucille
Horner visited us for a
while once on our house-
boat. Aunt Rose Byrd
lived in Memphis, Tenn-
essee. Lucille Horner
lived in Lobelville.

Archie Sayre and me
on Papa's birthday,
November 10, 1968, at
friends Willie Hughes
and his family at their
cabin on Brodie Road.

John Doyle caught big buffalo by trot line in Tennessee River. Doyle lived in Tom Creek and come to stop at our place on Click Creek for Papa to sell his fish to fish market in Jackson, Tennessee.

▶

Mrs. Vi Wolfe held big catfish that weighed 80 pounds. It was caught on October 17, 1961 by her husband Ben. Caught near Click Creek.

Elaine, Roy, and Lemo,
May, 1969

▶

Willie Hughes and his
wife Laula and Roy and
his wife Elaine at their
camp on Brodie Road

52

Archie Sayre caught big
turtle on a trot line in
Tennessee River at Click
Creek. The people are
our friends and they like
to hold turtle on stick in
the picture for fun.
1961.

▶

Louise's girl, July 1969

We would always have
a lot of trouble in
February and March
with rains. It would
rain so much, really too
much. This is the dog-
house. Sometimes we
would lose things during
floods. We tried to hold
onto things but you can
see right here there's a
pail and some other
things we tried to put
up and put away.
My dog Butch was on
the houseboat. But his
house flooded.

Sometimes the floods
made good fishing.
You'd have to move the
nets from one place to
another. You couldn't
leave them where it was
because the flood would
make the water so high
and the current would
be very strong and you'd
have to move them clos-
er to the land. And set
them up closer in. But
it was very good fishing.
The crappie, you could
get a lot at that time.
You couldn't have that
because of the game
warden. You reel them
in [with rod and reel].
But not in nets.

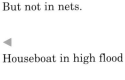

Houseboat in high flood

I took this for the same reason I took all the pictures—I really enjoy having them. And to show that there were two places to keep live fish.

If it was really cold he would get all dressed up in the little boat and he'd have two sets of overalls on and he had a fire in a little pail and gloves. And he'd go out fishing in the cold. He had on hip boots. Winter 1961-62

The ice has covered all over. All the river is ice. And my father would chop it. You couldn't walk on the ice, you'd go right through it. My father would stand on the edge and chop on the ice. What he's doing is he's breaking up the ice because it was scraping against the side of the boat. Winter 1961-62

Roy Lanier, one of Papa's friends and another man, helping my father. That's his boat in the background.

▶

This is my father Archie Sayre. He was just about to leave and I asked him to wait so I could take this picture before he went off and sold this batch of fish. So I convinced him to wait. And he took these and sold them. There were catfish in there and buffalo and carp in there, and some spoon-bill maybe. But he took the fish and sold them. He went to Robert Haynes' shop in Jackson, Tennessee. I made that dip net. There was a flood. You can see it in the tree line. Pretty much every year it would flood.

Sometimes it was pretty good fishing when the water was high. You can see there all the good fish.

This is my father washing the nets with a brush. Had to get the lines clean because they were dirty. They had leaves stuck in them. After we did that we'd bring in more nets that had to be washed. And then we'd hang them between two trees and we'd let them hang there until maybe the next day. Sometimes we'd be dipping them in tar. We had a big barrel that we would use. My father would stand there and we'd use a stick to stir the net while it was in the tar. We'd do that for maybe two or three minutes. And then we use a hook and I would put on gloves and hoist the net up into the air and use a stick to take them and made all the hot tar drip off and then we'd put those nets down on some wood plank and then we'd put another net in the tar. We might do twelve nets. My father would take them and hang them up on the trees—he would hold them in his hands far from his shoulder so he wouldn't get his clothes all dirty and he'd hang them between two trees on some nails. And we had more of them hanging all over the trees. And then we'd let them dry a day or two and we used rubber gloves to pick them up and take them over to the houseboat and get them all stacked up and ready. And we'd tie a rope on them and before my father would take them out he would get a drink of water and take them out in his small boat and set them up. I wouldn't go out in the small boat. I would stay on the houseboat and wash the snag lines, get them ready, or get whatever I had to get ready for the next run. And he would go out and set the lines. Put the nets down.

This is my father fixing a net. This is one already finished. When it's ready we'll put it in the dye. See him fixing it there. And then we'll dip it. These are things he kept off there and kept them away in case there was a flood. We just kept them away. The board there is to walk across.

I stood there and I shot this picture from up here. I was on the boat and looking that way. I shot the picture because I liked the picture. It was afternoon. It wasn't a job he did in mornings. In the mornings he took care of the fish that were in the river. He did that in the mornings. This was an afternoon job.

Archie Sayre and friend
in river landscape

There are no people
here. We put that cover
on the motor to protect
it from rain. There's a
carp and a big catfish.
There's one that's a buf-
falo [fish]. Another
carp. Down under
there's a spoonbill cat-
fish. Actually two
spoonbills.

My father hung them
like that, just hung
them on the hook, up
against each other. To
me, I see catfish. Two
catfish, side by side.
They're almost exactly
the same too. I told him
to fix it, I was going to
take the picture. I want-
ed to get that picture
before we sold these.

This is Pearl Dotson.
She was visiting. She
lives in Lobelville in
Tennessee which is near
Linden, Tennessee.
That's my father on the
porch. Maybe he's
touching his hat.
I was standing on land
when I snapped this
shot, looking at the boat
there. I think it's a good
picture. She was stand-
ing right there looking
when I snapped the
shot. I did snap it when
Pearl was ready to leave
and she went on home
then, back to Lobelville,
Tennessee.

Acknowledgments

Many people have contributed to this book. I appreciate and thank them all. First and foremost is Bob Fulcher, who over the past twelve years has accompanied, encouraged, and assisted me through his friendship and insight. Bobby gave me my first job as a documentary photographer and folklorist, and we were together the night I first met Maggie. His humor and intellect have been important to all the work I've done with Maggie. Jean Lindquist, who served as sign language interpreter for Maggie, me, and Bobby in Washington, DC, in 1986 at the Smithsonian's Festival of American Folklife, introduced me to the power of sign language and has continued as an interpreter for us. She has become a good friend and an important collaborator, indispensable in my relationship with Maggie Lee Sayre. Jean interpreted nearly all of the interviews with Maggie and many of Maggie's public presentations. These interpretations provide much of Maggie's original text in this book. With Jean around us Maggie and I can hear each other; for that we are both very grateful. Thanks also to Gallaudet University, Jean's employer, which has been interested in this story from the very beginning and hosted an exhibit of Maggie's photographs in 1987. A television crew from Gallaudet produced a segment about Maggie for "The Deaf Mosaic." The staff at the Decatur County Manor, particularly Shirley Collett and Beverly Montgomery, have taken an interest in Maggie and her photographs, and worked with us to arrange her travel to festivals and museum exhibitions.

A host of other people have helped push this project along. Mildred Middleton of Benton, Kentucky, provided significant information about Maggie and Kentucky School for the Deaf, and answered all my questions and letters with a gracious and poignant clarity. Barry Dornfeld and Allen Tullos assisted in two days of intensive video taped interviews with Maggie. Jens Lund's excellent scholarship on traditional river culture provided important context for my research. Ted and Pansy Sayre, Maggie's uncle and aunt, were gracious and helpful, providing background information on Archie Sayre and his family. The Southern Arts Federation supported a traveling exhibition of Maggie Lee Sayre's images from 1986-1989; Nancy Marshall printed many of Maggie Lee Sayre's negatives for exhibition. Robert Cogswell, Folk Arts Director at the Tennessee Arts Commission, frequently assisted Maggie in her participation at festivals. James B. Hardin of the American Folklife Center edited a shorter version of my introduction here for *Folklife Annual 1990* published by the Library of Congress. My colleagues at the Center for the Study of Southern Culture, University of Mississippi are forever supportive, and a faculty research grant from the College of Liberal Arts helped defray some costs of research. I must not forget to thank the two women on Brodie Road near Sugar Tree, Tennessee, who suggested that Bob Fulcher and I go to the local nursing home and visit Maggie Lee Sayre. They had the good sense and instinct to send us to the right place. Finally, nothing I do would ever get done without the patience and support of Ruthie, and our two fine boys, Julian and Alexander.

Obviously this could never have been a book without Maggie Lee Sayre and her compelling vision. Her willingness to share, her generosity of spirit, and her profound grace are just as impressive as her photographic vision. Her warmth, kindness, artistic gift, and strength of character are uncommon. The most satisfactory part of all has been the chance to spend time with Maggie, to laugh with her, and to learn just some of what she knows.

Library of Congress
Cataloging-in-Publication Data

Sayre, Maggie Lee, 1920-
"Deaf Maggie Lee Sayre" : photographs of a river life /
edited, and with an introductory essay, by Tom Rankin.
    p.   cm.
    ISBN 0-87805-788-9 (cloth : alk. paper).—
ISBN 0-87805-799-4 (paper : alk. paper)
    1. River life—Ohio River—Pictorial works. 2. River
life—Tennessee River—Pictorial works. 3. Riverboats—
Ohio River—Pictorial works. 4. Riverboats—Tennessee
River—Pictorial works. 5. Sayre, Maggie Lee, 1920-   —
Pictorial works. 6. Deaf—Ohio River—Pictorial works.
7. Deaf—Tennessee River—Pictorial works. 8. Ohio
River—Social life and customs—Pictorial works. 9.
Tennessee River—Social life and customs—Pictorial
works.
I. Rankin, Tom. II. Title.
F457.03S29 1995
976.8'052'092—dc20
[B]   95-4458
                                                            CIP

British Library Cataloging-in-Publication data available

Media Center (Library)
Elizabethtown Community College
Elizabethtown, KY 42701